ALL THAT
AND A BAG OF
NEURONS

Carly Bryson

NeoPoiesisPress.com

NeoPoiesis Press, LLC

2775 Harbor Ave SW, Suite D, Seattle, WA 98126-2138
Inquiries: Info@NeoPoiesisPress.com
NeoPoiesisPress.com

All That and a Bag of Neurons
ISBN 978-0- 9903565-4-7 (pbk)
        1. Poetry. I. Bryson, Carly.

Library of Congress Control Number: 2015919386

First Edition

Cover Design: Milo Duffin and Stephen Roxborough

Printed in the United States of America.

for Gordon

Contents

Without Grace

time was our hunger
  gnawing holes into our stomachs
  the fence waiting to be jumped
  the walls melting into us
  the drab days of no light
  the silence at the table of dysfunction
  the long stare into empty glass
  the terrain un-greened
  the imprint of hard dirt and bitterweed
  the longing for morning rain or distant seas
  the white noise of open windows
  the same, the same disappearing sun
collapsed, the graceless dreams

Spring Redux

spring is one season closer to hibernation
the rain will lend a month of flowers
to the premature heat of april
we'll cherish the cool night
committing the chill to memory
we'll wonder why man doesn't die sooner
one gentle breeze at a time

Still Life with Background Noise

the death of love begins
with the roll of the eye
the imperceptible sneer
the twitch at the side of the mouth
the question tossed aside
the subject changed

if the disintegration of bones
is the body preparing to die
then the light that sputters and sparks
no longer charging the air
is the precursor to a lonely epitaph

Ghosts by Other Names

she called her ghosts by other names
the dead child who never surfaced
the outstretched hand
shooting agates down the hallway
the cedar box with snapshots
of people long forgotten
the mid-century chest
where memories were neatly folded
with school papers and greeting cards
thousand hour days spent cutting quilt scraps
and hoarding buttons
formless shadows only visible
in the light of the gas stove
hands pockmarked from picking cotton
the bent back and lasting scars
the stone dog she tripped over
her broken hip
the ironing board where every shirt was dampened
and steam ironed to perfection
the dead child, the lost child, the dead husband
the prodigal daughter who left and never returned
the ashtray where she flicked her salvation

Bleak Town

when it came, it came
white rivers rushing down from frozen clouds
buttressing anything solid and vertical
feast or famine say the locals
one year it's nothing and the next it's nothing but
with undiluted weariness, old timers swear it's their last season
they can't even lift the shovels
they stay each year, each storms toss bringing whiter hair
the wrinkles more ruthless, the eyes less focused
outside the window, the bleakness is stark but temporary
waiting for the sun is a pastime, checkers on Thursday
barber shop fodder fished from the grist barrel

Grace in Remission

beneath these veils
and we all wear them
below the neckline
beneath the rasp and sigh
there caressing the skin
the life cycle of a silkworm
woven mother's milk
criss-crossing the hip
a vermillion whisper
grace in remission

Let it Fly

there are too many words
resting on tree branches,
how many times can a willow weep?

too many analogies to birds
and passages stolen from folk remedies
apple cider vinegar cures everything
but sadly lacks as a muse

and water pure clear every blue hue
as it rolls down a hillside after a light rain
as it carves a gorge through canyons
as it calls every boy who craves the sea

give the people what they want
color each page carefully
embellish the sky with darkness
the grass is not wet but fecund

this is how you sell your soul
one illusion at a time
dropped on paper- inked dreams

make an airplane
fold it
let it fly

Dynastic Empire for the Win

Dynastic Empire for the win,
once ahead by a nose hair,
now mere steps from the finish.

They sprayed something in the air.
I could smell it, taste it and
my throat ached for two days.

We've arrived on Mars again,
when the ant farm implodes,
the queen must have a trajectory.

Friends are stockpiling
beans, rice, bullets.
The rest of us are waiting for payday

You can only sing Amazing Grace
so many times before you realize
no wretches will be saved.

No one left to wonder
why we kept all those old snapshots.

All That and a Bag of Neurons

somewhere on earth
a grain of sand is your dirt twin
brother from another other
don't confuse being a particle
with being a part of

we are little more than
pig's leavings and crow pickings

subversive compost carbon insurgents
we think therefore we think we are
drown us and we turn to silt
fetid on a summer's day

Twin Railways

We roar hollow
in opposing directions,
our tracks lie side by side
in separate dimensions.

Your window faces the sun,
the light through the glass
forms a kaleidoscope
of lavender fields and goldenrod.

Mine looks out at the night sky,
speed blurs constellations
into light freckles on indigo canvas.

We meet on the platform
stepping from fire pools and ice ponds,
touching only because we have to.

Dirt Ghosts

i am stitched together
loosely so the air gets in
this is not flesh but filament
hen leavings and raven pickings
tendon streamers gored sallow
anchored to bone
buoyed by god-seeds
it will take dirt ghosts
to unravel these threads

Unfinished

That old house haunts me,
we left it all unfinished.

Daddy's sign shop in the back,
paint stacked on every shelf,
where he spent cold winters at his easel
warmed by a gas space heater.
If the place had ever caught fire
the neighborhood would have been in flames.

The root cellar where we hid as kids
holding séances and reading comic books
had spiders and dirt walls but we didn't care.
It suited our quest for things of wonder--
a womb outside of the womb.

The clothesline stretched across the yard
where Mama hung clothes washed in alkaline water.
The sun dried them so stiff,
we almost had to bend them to fit in the basket.

The tiny living room with the sectional
where six of us gathered around the Magnavox,
and neighbor boys would come practice guitars
because our mom was the only one who allowed it.

The garage I wretched behind
cursing God when our kid brother died.
After that, the house grew smaller,
smothered by our collective grief.

We left and moved on,
some sooner than others.
Then it was just Mama
rattling around the kitchen,

sitting at her sewing machine
and quilting squares until her fingers bled.

After she died, I realized that house was
where we left everything,
unfinished lives, unfinished dreams
and the ghosts of what remained.

Like Dust Devils

they told her he didn't mean it
he saw worms crawling from his skin
she was superfluous--apart but a part
and never had a memory of it
and wondered if it was why
she lost the connection with him later
when she was rebelling against it all
and his words held no meaning for her
when god left her those few years
when she cried out
and the sound flew into the distant air
rolling silent on a strong dry wind
like dust devils--assimilating spirits into their vortex
hers was gathered up and sucked into the momentum
the strong absorbing the weak
like that night when she innocently danced in the maelstrom
lost in the story within the story
stored in the mind file for another place and time

Leviathan

bind in leatherette
metal on mettle
brass on silk
i see through you
goggled eyes
x-rayed you shine
your radium spine
flesh of a phosphorescent nothing
eviscerate me leviathan
mechanical hearts don't weep

Freak Storm

The car dies in the middle of Weslayan.
It's not natural for this desert child to drown in the rain
or slosh knee deep in water that shouldn't be green
and full of gasoline and fire ants.

I step from the car, and it's cold in January,
these poor hypothermic limbs will never be the same,
blue from toe to meniscus.

Missing my dirt today,
hard cracked and solid beneath my boots.
Even if the sun cries sometimes,
its tears only make sparks.

January

January swallows the remainder of winter.
Days fill with gray, white, fog and dust
but writing about weather is almost as boring
as talking about weather--
How much can be said that hasn't been said?

Spring renews, summer is hot, fall is brown
and winter is cold.

Now--let's talk about you or me or dead armadillos,
or how looking at cracked paint too long can be Godlike,
or how your boss has Chia pet hair and Chupacabra eyes,
or how the world is on the brink of collapse,
but we will never see it coming
because we can't see beyond twenty four hours.

A Perfect Reason for Silence

It's the need that is the curse of it all.
Words aren't born from want,
they would just jumble the mind,
fingers would burn at a touch of the temple.
And what of those with no hands, no eyes, no voice?
Need then becomes a beautiful tragedy.
A perfect reason for silence.

Faith in Finding the Right Words

Some words could sell redemption to Satan,
turn anarchy to salvation.
I don't possess them.
Someday by osmosis they will be there,
when I'm scratching around like a grackle in gravel,
searching for a seed only to find a discarded Dorito.
I have faith.
I.Have.Faith.

November Redux

November you have foiled me again,
despite my love for your crackly leaves
and brisk wind.
you have managed once again
to stress me right before the holidays.

Perhaps it's not you.
Perhaps Jupiter is not aligned
with my seventh house of luck,
or my Neptune is trined or some such.
Surely there is a reason.

I give you my love, my imagination,
my wonder of all beauty.
You give me bounced paychecks,
a runny nose and forgotten bills.

It will take me until July,
when I begin my yearly craving to forget.
By then my brain will be baked from the sun
and of course I will again forgive you.

Static-in-Motion

I hide in folded corners
resisting the "truth is stranger than fiction"
of me.

Concealed here amongst the crowd
daring myself to stand out,
deer in the headlights,
shrinking in the commotion.

In the largesse, I slink away
becoming a caricature,
a microcosm of myself
so small that ants loom
THEM-ish, and I too mutate
in the glare of a rogue sun.

Too inconsequential to ignite.
Too vital to dissolve.
I remain in contradiction.
Static-in-motion.

Little Killers of the Working Class

Girls running on hormonal excess, fresh out of wisdom, we lived in the land of men, mean boys and roughnecks, midnight parties on oil lease land with washtubs of beer in caliche pits above beds of sylvite and potash. We had to be as tough as them or they would just take what we wouldn't give. On weekends we drove to the Pecos, a watery mud prison in the middle of nothing, the anti-oasis, a wet hole in the desert's belly.

The first time I sank in it up to my thighs, but that's what we did. One hundred miles of nowhere in any direction. Our choices were slim. The place was solemn, buzzards circled in formation overhead. If you listened long enough there was scrabbled beauty in the wind.

At night the moon swam on the water. We watched coyotes scuttle in the brush, and the boys all had rifles in their trucks--little killers of the working class.

We drove sixty miles back to our living rooms--Ed Sullivan, Mama's Goulash served on Melmac, and air filled with the smell of Daddy's pipe.

Letting Go

we felt it rather than heard it
the hair rising on our napes
the sickening rush of adrenaline
the quick glance around the room
an innate search for shelter

the sun shone slats across the wood floor
in retrospect a trivial observance
but the last normal thing we saw

the ceiling gave way to daylight
grout popped out of tiles
sending them into the air as ceramic missiles
the floor cracked down the middle

we scurried to a hall closet
covering ourselves with old pillows
and winter blankets

we thought about sunny days
simple pleasures and morning walks

we didn't talk   our breathing was too loud
we didn't touch   our skin was burning
resolve melted into sighs
the resignation of the damned
that moment when it's too late for prayers
and too soon for absolution

we were the waking dead for hours
until finally with breath hot on our faces
whispered that it was okay to let go

I Keep Thinking There is Something That Will Move Me

I keep thinking there is something that will move me beyond what I am or what I have been, a meteor to fall to earth and single me out.

I see it coming and jerk away just a millimeter to the left of where it lands, dangerously close to the crater, the smoldering earth laps at my feet, the ground gives way, sucking me down into the vortex, but I find a sturdy shrub and hold fast, pulling myself up and away.

It never happens that way, life begins and ends lying in bed either trying to wake up or trying to go to sleep. Nothing in between matters if nothing ever changes.

They Tell Me It Is Not the Time for Frivolity

They tell me it is not the time for frivolity,
one mustn't make jokes or take anything less than seriously.

So I revisit Sun Tzu and Castaneda, preparing my warrior self,
though I hate planting, preparing my soil, reworking my stratagem.

I won't stand in the street with a sign, the time for signs has passed.
I won't utter a sound bite, the time for talk has passed.

In my mind I am ninja. I can slither over tall gates,
land quietly on my feet, and walk through doors unseen.

I am the survivor with the gas mask and the sodium iodide
lurking in a hidden forest watching over my clan.

The thought makes me giggle to the point of not breathing.
I am a silly woman who has lived a little, and that may have to be enough.

Younger, I Viewed the World Through Diamond Eyes

Younger, I viewed the world through diamond eyes. The tall sunflowers grew wild along the red dirt shoulders of my desert home. Their bright petals burst straight from the earth straining to paint the sky gold.

On the beaches in Jacksonville, each piece of driftwood was the shape of art. The sand wasn't white like Fort Walton, but the sight of the sun rising red in the morning sold the sparkling waves of the Atlantic. In the evenings, fishermen would dock their boats at the marina, and their wives would fry grouper served with cornbread and beer.

Later, it was New Orleans where the shine began to dim. It was easy to love the history, the narrow French Quarter streets, the riverfront wharfs, the steamboats, steepled cathedrals and sidewalk cafes. But other things had changed my viewpoint. The women who walked the alleys off Bourbon, the hoo-doo ladies who peered out of front doors with vacant stares, the girl-boys groping each other behind Club LaFitte, the men who grabbed me as I looked in store windows, being lifted off my feet during a Mardi Gras throng.

No judgment, it was another world, but it made the bright yellow road flowers of home seem far away and forever gone. The beauty that had once filled me abandoned me, leaving what was left of me erased and grown older before my time.

Chains at the Gate

they are clanging their chains at the gate
clinking across the macadam
souls melt and flow into culverts
the voices of many scream

smelly boys go home to your beds
have a nice cup of mama's tea
fill your flat bellies with bread

the dark night is far from over
in fact it has just began

Sometimes I Miss the Sea

Sometimes I miss the sea
the saline sepulcher that sneezes
to form rain on the shores of man.

Out of molecules and photons
come blue- green infusions from the sun.

I want to roll across whitecaps
until I reach a glassy cove,
where I can view the world as it began.

Waiting for Rain

I was once edgy
knife tips for fingers
blood as dark as adder's milk
bitter among the avant garde
had to stay a step ahead
so i could laugh at them
dressed in tunics and slim pants
owl pendants and cranberry hair
full of sarcasm and snide
fell to earth landing in a puke bucket
face first into the dirt
but i've always come clean in the rain

Burned Away

I see images of flames
dancing around the trees we sat near,
the oak, the pecan, the cedar and pine.

Those strong silhouettes stood shadowed
beneath a ballet of stars in the evening sky.

In the quiet nothing, we talked, drank, loved,
legs dangled from the river's edge,
moon's eyes adrift on the water.

Now red and umber reflect from the hills,
earth shrouded in charcoal.
How quickly it all crumbles
when the world has burned away.

Ashes on the Inside

The heat has beaten me.
I am melting on the inside,
blood boiled like a Lafayette crawfish.

This is how the dinosaurs died,
it wasn't the ice, it was the fire.
The world began burning
and didn't stop for a thousand years.

Fossils aren't petrified bones
they are imprints kiln fired into the earth

That's how they will find me
resting in a shallow grave of dirt and soot.

Languishing Away in the Big Fried Empty

Sneezing ocotillo dust
as it whispers in on a west wind
smelling of lavender and creosote
and tasting like spit.

Eyes close para minuto,
I pretend to smell rain.
Sweet ozone lingers for a second
but only in a memory.

Eight months since the last boomer.
No use bartering with the devil
for things that can never be.

A crush of whisky tinted mesas
line the end of the world,
and I'm so very tired.

I sing to stay awake
to keep from thinking.
Thinking brings thoughts,
thoughts bring ideas,
ideas mean notes,
notes mean pulling over.

I crave something cold,
or a mulberry, a succulent something.

In the vastness of this empty,
where sky swallows land,
my only burdens are miles and hours.

I want to stop and stretch,
stand in the sunflowers,
let the rattlers taste my boots.

I've lived among living things too long,
long enough to get weary,
long enough to crave this dry Texas dirt,
this dead dead bottom of a dried up sea.

Worms

People keep chanting for change.

Nothing will change without understanding the roots.
Innovation and greed combined to change the world,
long before you came and will continue when you're gone.
The same people you trusted sold you out, and it was easy.

Change isn't a picket line--it's retching your guts out.
Regurgitating the lies you swallowed,
year after year, decade after decade.
Even now you're choking on them.
They move in your intestines like tapeworms

Sing it, pray it, write it, speak it
until you swallow yourself whole.

If you aren't the change you are the lie.
You are the worm.

A Sundial in Shadow

Dustbowl days and suicides
the ground gave up three months ago
cracks, deep reveals of middle Earth
the cattle, complacent bags of bones
too sick to milk, too thin to slaughter
no rain for grass, no grass for hay
oh for a sun dial in shadow
an afternoon zephyr, a cloud filled day
a storm in the morning, drench the hedgerows
soak the Indian corn, wash away the rotters
fill the creeks, irrigate the glades
of sweet deliverance, we have no choice
die along with it or just pray

Muse in Effigy

Muse you burn in effigy
strung tight from a bridge rail
in the sun's late zenith
poached Narcissus
reflection flapping in the blue-green swill

I'll borrow your carcass
hold it in the mind bank
to dust off someday
I'll polish your stone countenance
and air out your death smell
until you are beautiful once more

Tomorrow

No water for the pails while we burn
the river is dry and the townsmen sleeping
we'll hide beneath the sheets
to dream of pleasant things
tomorrow is always tomorrow

Dear Desert

I gave you tender feet to
plant your caltrop
blood offerings to redden your dirt
scaled your mesas of scalp and sage
swallowed your gusts of alkaline wind
you taunted me with rain shadows
while I drowned in the bone dust
of outlaws and myth

Hear

Sparrows huddle into bird clans on the wire
perched silhouettes stark against the sky.

His fingers dig into the fleshy part of your arm.
you want to extract them with pliers
pluck each knuckle one at a time.

A tool shed exclamation
is something He would hear.

Where Did You Go, Landis Everson?

You swam in wild honey
before the bees started dying.

It's my prognosis that confusing
herself for a black widow,
the queen selfishly devoured them.

I think you only reappeared in dreams
to deliver your own eulogy.

It was time, and time
was the only thing missing.

The voice lies embedded,
the sky is still blue,
and at least we have that.

Wings

Sweep the floor, butterfly,
until the dirt disappears,
replaced with the sheen
of wrecked devotion.

You were left to gnaw open
your own worth,
to chip your teeth
on a bottle of time.

Those wings are tethered loosely
but not loose enough to fly.

Some Things I Know

I didn't question why green grass only grew on other people's
lawns.

I knew that no matter how often we swept the floor was still gritty
and the window sills were full of sand blown in by the last north
wind.

I knew the Pyracantha that flourished on the side of the house
produced white blossoms in spring and orange berries in fall,
and the cedar in the back yard left sharp needles for bare feet.

I knew we found occasional rattlesnake skins hanging from elms
during the molting season and that black tarantulas jump--
but not twenty feet. I knew building makeshift forts and dollhouses
was easy on hard dirt, and clotheslines made excellent target
holders.

I knew storm cellars were as much sanctuary as shelter
and we sat in that hole with roots growing from the walls,
holding séances and trading comic books. We never once
went down there for a tornado.

Roll

the heat shimmer-waves of summer begin
fingers of light bounce from pavement
rubber sticks to painted lines
hesitant at each curve a drive through
oasis thrives in the space
where blacktop meets air
our blackpool eyes fix on the straightaway
our feet are made of tumbleweeds
we roll and roll with the thistle and gravel
until day turns into creosote night
waves conflate into tar and we are coolness

Forsaken

forsaken: abandoned (someone or something)

After, we gathered what few wits afforded us by genetic memory
and loaded them into the wheelbarrows with the rest of the
refuse, another trip to the junkyard of forsaken lives.

Every curb on every street was piled high with remnants of the
recent past, and the mattresses struck us the hardest, private
fortresses caked with mud, memories gone in minutes, flashes of
stolen kisses lying in a trash heap.

Something that was once an avenue was now a rutted trail,
asphalt was carried far by the rain, a river of tiny rocks. Even the
dirt smelled of mold, and the mold smelled of decay.

We avoided looking out to sea after the dark was unleashed. Later,
it was as shiny as glass, a black lagoon, a gray reminder filled with
ghosts, and the ghosts weren't talking.

Trestle

near the trestle
thistles birth babies beneath the tracks
the wind scatters the seeds
populating sand banks with weeds that never grow
they just rest there bonzaied naked in the sun
until the next norther picks them up
and flies them down to mexico on dirt wings

Conquered

Weather here is feast or famine,
we are either burnt into crispy shell people,
macaroni craft projects shaped like humans,
held together by paste, glossed over with shellac,
or it rains for days until the ground begins
holding the grass hostage.

Of course it gives us something to talk about,
dialogue without borders,
the only controversy being who to blame,
nature or God.

It affects us all, bridging political and social gaps,
maybe it's (nature or God's) way of telling us something
that our slowly evolving minds have yet to grasp.

Maybe those aren't raindrops but iridescent eyes,
and the sun only beats down to teach us what it's like
to feel conquered.

Gristle and Bone

Maybe I'll go
where unspoiled minds go
before ideas become atrophied
from the weight of ego
and the movement of years

before the loss of words
becomes as simple
as the cut of a cord
the finding solace in endless wombs
each one a sad surrogate
for serenity

before I curl into these limbs
these barren stalks
this skin that never sheds
because it has been reduced
to a sheath, a window
of gristle and bone

Controlled Opposition

you thought it was your luck
the stars were against you
kismet   fate aligned
to thwart your plans
your skin is not flesh but stone
the remnants of an ancient obelisk
struck by the lightning of gods
animated to motion
and you move like a marionette
one arm up one down
legs akimbo
dancing at the whim of another

Laws of Reflection

I see you moon, always lurking,
drafting off the stars, clutching the pretense of light,
laughing at my little human tragedies.

In retrospect I should have climbed that tree,
reached out and clutched your sullen light
and wiped the smirk right off your face.

Like the time you gloated when I was twenty-eight
and all my power was sucked into the vortex
of age and responsibility.

You knew I would birth a life that needed saving
when I could barely even save my own.

The Dad You Never Knew

how he describes the brush smoothing the horse hair
the way the sunlight skims across a certain spot on the creek
the part that still has water
the way he folds life into the dullest topic
so that no one falls asleep
how he paints pebbles on the beach
not just beige rocks but unvarnished gemstones
how his voice is never shrill, a well-oiled hum
and dust doesn't touch him but floats around his perimeter
intimidated by his boundaries and his dark stays within night
never corroding the day

Regret

Too late for dinner,
I ate that sin earlier in the day,
choked down with a poison soda.

Each day I swallow a new regret,
they go down surprisingly smooth,
a raw oyster sliding down the throat.

Somewhere between the esophagus and the stomach
the gag reflex kicks in.
Regret stays down and slithers through the core,
coating each gut part with aches of memory.

It lies there brick-like,
each particle attaching to the helix.
A guaranteed reflux somewhere
between this life and the next.

Ride

I rode out the dirt clouds into nothing that mattered,
into tornado tracks in an empty field of mud ruts.

I was a nomad armed with skunk weed,
pragmatism wrapped in poetry.

I pitied those heifers lying upside down in the culvert,
the lone victims of a dry squall, with their low pitiful bellowing
and their spindly legs braced against the wind.

Day to Night

south of here where
the pines are replaced by cypress
wheat replaced by winter oats
action replaced by inertia
lunatics feel the moon wane
while lying in striped hammocks
bleached pastel from the sun
tipping beer cans onto the san augustine
foam for the ants and dog fodder
the only thing that changes is the calendar page
day turns to night
light to dark
fingers curl around cheap cigars
smoke rings around the sun
the cloud particles of change
don't come around often
and when they do
no one really cares

Pink Flamingos

i didn't want to watch your dad till rows
of corn and sweet potatoes
but i watched him dig them up day after day
orange gold in the afternoon sun
something had drawn me off the road
away from the austin lights
into the pine trees and azaleas
into the winding red dirt
into the forest of lost causes
where old men still plow their fields
and collapse under the weight of simple dreams
where wives still blanch the picked corn
stock up the deep freeze
rake infinite twigs and needles
and plant pink flamingos in the yard

Pictures of Summer

Summer.
Several heat strokes later, I can say I never liked it.
Snowcones. Sugar, water, ice.
I always liked the blue ones and the resulting Smurf tongues
that grace every color photo of me from childhood,
except the one where I placed an entire boiled egg
in my mouth and smiled.
Summer. I blame the heat.

In Dark Hours

Give me dark hours or moments,
a brief reprieve from the sirens
and helicopters maneuvering through clouds,
cars honking below my office window,
with double bass woofers that rattle the panes.
I should be able to tune them out,
relegate them to that subconscious place
reserved for nagging voices and rotten odor,
file thirteen located just behind the mind's eye.
Things that auto filter into synaptic containment.
Leave them to bathe in their own vapor trails,
locked in a cage labeled un-loved and un-lovely.
Let them sleep while I ponder.

Cloudbursts

Someday I'll leave this dark air.
These cloudbursts that enter my mouth
hang low in my throat and stay there until
the first cup of coffee pretends to cleanse
but lodges whatever refuse rose from the ground.

Somewhere between the heart and gut,
wet fragments of death fingers
wait to be whole, wait for the signal.
Angels with checkered flags, a thumbs up.

They wrap around each chakra until slowly
they diminish and the soul ceases.
It drifts upward like smoke
to replenish the dead sky.

Skies of Leaden Dreams

life has beaten every metaphor from my bones
and ground the marrow into dustmeal
somewhere the words got lost
on a long highway between the ocotillo and kudzu
between the ghost towns and tractor graveyards
where dry yellow grass gave way
to the oppression of overgrowth
between endless drought and sudden squalls
where memories were scattered in the dirt
or callously washed away
only to be recollected by stars on a clear night

Invisible

light slices through me like a ghost machete
you can only touch what you can see
those aren't flames singeing your fingers
but memories freed from a fire-proof box
soon to be drowned in rivulets of forget-me-rain
the kind that drenches the seed stock
until the roots are too shallow to stand
when the clouds dissipates the blade retreats
back into a child's dream that never really mattered

Misfired

I have no words to paint souls
the colors of prisms
or inspire dreams of deep love
and revolutions
even muted brilliance is still brilliant
and this shell is primered clay
left out of the kiln
waiting for the subconscious
to become whole and unstained
but those neurons are gone
misfired on a summer day

Unique

your salt is barren
devoid of everything but the taste
like the wasteland
the long ago bottom of an ancient sea
dredged for gold plated skeletons
bones haphazardly rearranged by time
in a million years our marrow will be the silt
dragonflies will still hover
gulls will skim the whitecaps
blue will acquiesce to the fertile sludge
of whispering ghosts
and you were thinking you were unique

My Mind is a Ghost Town

my mind is a ghost town
long abandoned
nothing left but
old railroad tracks
with missing ties

my mind is a cheap motel
with blue metal chairs
and a wanda jackson poster
sitting on a dirt road near tucumcari
where even the weeds cry

my mind is an old impala
sleeping in its own rust
its back seat stories
ended in the crisp brown hills
sacrificed to the dust and wind

Silence

Bathe in silence, it comforts
it washes ruined words clean
and sterilizes re-opened wounds.
It allows the thinking mind to breathe
in quiet echoes, the message unheard
but no one listens anymore.

In the Heat of Things

In the heat of things I am quietly
hibernating in the shade,
beyond the solar flares.
Break your shovels in the hard dirt,
I'll sit by the window waiting for rain
to stain the metal roof,
like ink on an empty page.

Once

the world was covered in a veil of flowers
a light bulb melted
morphing into the face of someone I knew
an olive oyl of a girl
all limbs and teeth
we talked as if the world was normal
while war played on the radio

Flown

i am bent backward
weed in the wind
lotus center
suspended midair
i belly crawl
in the silver dusk
curl into the earth
this soft machine
dust-swaddled bed of bones

A Ton of Bricks

days blow through time like seed pods
flowering for the sun folding under the cold moon
that one stretch is all you'll get as your bones feel the impact
of a thousand mornings and a thousand rains
don't think or you'll shatter like marbles in a blender
bend into the black light sleep while you sleep
things can go wrong so just lie there knee deep in the muck
leaning into the shadows like a ton of bricks on linen

Note from a January Night

White room, its cleanliness negotiable.
Your room faces the southern sky,
great for African Violets I've heard.
I think I won't remember that musing.
I'll remember the ventilator tube, the feeding tube,
the tubes running inside your arms and orifices.
I clean the plastic tubing when no one is looking.
I rewash the lavatory and door handles.
I pray in silence when your eyes are closed
because I know you can hear me.
I hold your hand, the long thin artistic fingers,
and wonder when you found time to grow older,
when you went from boy to man.
I still see a cherub face turned gaunt from liquid feedings.
The boy now too big to hold, and I know you would hate that.
My mind is cluttered with the talk of brain scans and catheters,
transfusions and prognosis, rehab and recovery.
Your bedside buzzes with nurses and aides,
doctors and med students,
bubble boy without the bubble.
I place an iPod on your pillow in case it's true that music
stimulates the brain to recover.
I make silent deals with God.
I make silent deals with Satan.
When I leave at night I recite Buddhist chants in the car,
to cover every base, to calm myself.
My mind is on auto pilot,
I don't sleep or eat.
I go to your apartment and clean it,
I clean the inside of your car.
I give the ten spot in your wallet to a homeless man,
in case karma can be purchased.
I grab some gym clothes for when you go to therapy.
I don't lose hope, though I am frightened beyond reason.
I whisper fight mantras in your ear.

I whisper tales of hope and regeneration.
I whisper tales of Icarus and wings that never fail.
Tonight you grabbed my hand.
Tonight you opened your eyes.
Tonight I understood determination.
Tonight maybe I will sleep.

Breached

Let me tell you about the hibiscus that sits below the bedroom window, how it reaches for the sun in the morning, how its stem elongates like a lover's neck stretched in yearning. I'll tell you about the blue sky on a crisp December day, how it's only marred by ribbons of clouds and how when you squint they resemble a wispy necklace encircling the sun. Then there is the truth of it. How the air is littered with the dirty particles of progress. How machines circle the parameters of the city, a formation of whirs and hums. Flying eyes with laser vision, invasive enough to rattle the quiet reminder that the throbbing you hear is not the blood racing through your arteries but a breach of solitude, a rift in the silence of things.

The Silence of Air

the silence of air
must live in a dimensional pathway
a light saber of quiet rescue
that slices through the noise of motion
beyond the whisper of hope
and the gospel of breathing
where even heartbeats
that ripple up through the chest
find shelter in the stillness

Flee

how we let the world consume us
we are renewable-- soylent green
we are flesh crackers on two legs
even animals know when to flee

Acknowledgements

Some of these poems have been published in various journals, collections, and e-zines including:

Red Fez: "All That and a Bag of Neurons", "Twin Railways"
The Montucky Review: "Ashes on the Inside"
My Favorite Bullet: "Once"
Killpoet: "Flown"
Vext: "The Silence of Air", "Flee"

About the Author

Carly Bryson lives in Houston, Texas and writes poetry and prose about cracked dirt, the desert, lonesome highways, dirty rotten wars, nasty city air, pending dystopia and the frailty of the human condition.

NeoPoiesis: *a new way of making*

1) in ancient Greece, poiesis referred to the process of making: creation - production - organization - formation - causation

2) a process that can be physical and spiritual, biological and intellectual, artistic and technological, material and teleological, efficient and formal

3) a means of modifying the environment and a method of organizing the self, the making of art and music and poetry, the fashioning of memory and history and philosophy, the construction of perception and expression and reality

4) an independent publisher with a steadfast goal to print and promote outstanding poets, writers and artists that reflect the creative drive and spirit of the new electronic landscape

NeoPoiesisPress.com